Giving Ground

GIVING GROUND

Poems by
Lynn M. Knapp

*For Miriam:
Your bright spirit
inspires me!*

Lynn K

A Publication of The Poetry Box®

Library of Congress Control Number: 2016953119

ISBN-13: 978-0-9863304-9-0
ISBN-10: 9863304-9-3

Published by The Poetry Box®, 2017
Beaverton, Oregon
www.ThePoetryBox.com
530.409.0721

For my teachers:

my neighbors and my students

TABLE OF CONTENTS

One

Two

Three

Four

❈ ❈ ❈

One

EXIT
35
M P H

*a ribbon
of heedless
life . . .*

Welcome to the Neighborhood

He blows whiskey breath
and a slurred invitation
over the fence,
*Whydoncha come over
and play cards?*
I hesitate.
Doncha play cards?
I picture a bent, bandy-legged,
cigarette-burned card table,
slick with white ashes,
sticky with booze.
Sorry, I don't.

La Casa de Mis Bisabuelos

They would think it strange
to hear me say it,
an old carpenter with broken hands
and a railroad pension,
a cross old woman who smoked
a corncob pipe and spoke
a few words of childhood German,
rocking together on the same front porch
I pass today.

A full-blooded *casa* now,
the house Great-Grandpa built
wears aqua-blue paint,
has white plastic chairs under the carport,
a Rottweiler on a chain,
pink flamingos stepping lightly
over the flowerbeds,
and a backyard mechanic
draped over a fender
with his ear
to a squawking fan belt.

Odd Couplings

A black rabbit scans the meadow,
ears rotating like radar.
Couplings spark steel-on-steel
between boxcars,
rolling billboards
for gangsters who paint
fat, horizon-high letters
in the dark of night.

Traffic pulses like surf on the four-lane,
trucks rumble down Vine,
the pathway ahead
threading between them,
a ribbon of heedless life,
grass greening cracks in the asphalt,
blue-brown quail nestled in brush
under falling rain.

A hardy strain of rabbits,
born when a lop-eared pet
took a cottontail bride,
slumber beneath parked cars,
dodge hungry vagrants, trucks, and cats.
At dusk, rabbits reclaim
the railroad meadow,
cropping grass like deer,
grazing in silken quiet
on the freeway hillside.

GOLDEN EYE

I sprint up the wildwood hill,
snowy path stretching ahead—
tic-tac-toe of animal and human,
cat, dog, Nike tread,
magpie alighting,
running steps of rabbit.
A solitary pheasant, a young male,
clatters out of the brush,
flying alongside me
until his fear is spent.

Perhaps he is lost,
separated from his family
or in search of one.
A slim brown hen
scuttles into the undergrowth.
The rooster is not searching for a hen—
he has found her
and shelters her in the thick brush
on a snowy slope of the freeway.

As I crest the hill,
not one trim brown hen,
but two run at my approach.
There he is again, that handsome devil,
turning a golden eye toward me,
lifting emerald head and crimson throat,
leading flight to a brown-twigged hill
across the rusty railroad track.

I stop, breathe deep,
hear the rattle of their wings,
sense the pounding of their hearts,
and count,
two, three, then four speckled hens
raising wings to follow him.

Goddamn English

Mario pats the couch beside him
in front of the TV,
but she chooses not to see,
lips mouthing harsh foreign
syllables as ideas and images
begin to flow,
and as a door opens for her
another closes between them.

Going On Three

Sofía understands Spanish
but watches TV in English.
She toys absently with a taco and beans,
sniffs a burrito, devours a Big Mac.
Too short for the counter,
she tugs Lorena's skirt,
Mommy, the man says
you need another penny.
Not for her, a conspicuous accent,
not for her, an ambiguous culture,
no linguistic confusion for her.
She understands Spanish
but answers in English.

Giving Ground

Casting nets of anemic,
translucent roots,
creeping bellflower burrows,
entrapping, encircling
roses, hostas, delphiniums,
dividing, branching, seeking.

I follow amazed, mesmerized.
I'm Alice down the garden rabbit hole.
I dig, I paw, possessed.
The roots have no end.

As the sun climbs in the sky,
I stagger to my feet,
leaning on a shovel to survey
wave on wave
of mute, unyielding green—
tenacious, deep-rooted,
in dust and loam alike.

Dangerous

In full fourteen-year bloom,
I shrank from unintelligible foreign chatter
of dark young men in grocery store aisles,
certain they were talking about me.
Now I teach young men who top onions
and pick cherries far away
from their families, young men who giggle
at young ladies without Mamá or Abuela
to scold them. They grip pencils in dim classrooms
at night, giving form to a new life with aching fingers.

HOUSE MOUSE

Drawn irresistibly
to a steamy scent of kitchen,
sweet underbelly of sink,
moist Shangri-La
ripe with cheese,
potato peels, egg shells,
and bacon fat,
he scampers
across a border
from his wintry home
to the tropic warmth
of mine, unaware
of a world where
an inhospitable trap
will snap his neck,
leaving him
curled in the lap
of my frosty garden,
black eyes still shining.

Esperanza

In the little house beside the tracks,
they struggle to feed a family of nine,
one more every year.

I trudge past, up the hill,
sweltering in the August heat
to see what can only be
a mirage—
Esperanza hanging laundry
under a windblown tree,
billowing yellow sheets,
roseate t-shirts,
tiny blue britches,
fluttering pink undies,
arcing like a rainbow
on an unexpected breeze.

GROWN-UP GANGSTERS

We take a walk in the evening,
and from tidy little yards,
they say *Hello* over the fence.

I've seen you before, they say.
You live over by Tino's Tacos.
You have a nice garden.

I know them when I see them,
watchful, macho, brawny in black,
slow to speak, slow to trust,
taut, folded biceps,
bulging beneath hacked-off sleeves.

We walk past, and they hoist
the babies to wave goodbye.
Grown-up gangsters know where we live.

HOMEBOY

He thinks he knows
what it means to be a man—
homemade tattoo, *12th Street*
above the eyebrow he cocks like a gun.

Hair slicked back, tie askew,
he flirts with the pretty woman
who asks him questions,
bragging about the others,
all the girls who wanted him
as his mother weeps.

At seventeen going on fourteen,
he thinks himself a lethal weapon
on the street, in the bedroom,
milk-toothed smile
beneath a downy mustache,
baby-faced tough guy
on his way to prison.
There he will cry for his mother,
there he will learn he's still a child.

Robin Spring

I see them fly over the sunken arbor,
limned in the cold eye of a setting sun.
They roost, red and ripe, a feathered tree of life,
studding branches of a barren tree.
One by one, open-winged
they glide to feast
on clusters of drooping fruit,
summer's sodden waste,
their harbor found
in my garden's untended shame.

Bleeding Heart

A strange green light
descends before the rain
as I track nettle vines
to their source,
shimmering, silver-backed usurpers
snaking on their bellies
through my Eden,
thriving in that short space
of hesitation,
a gardener's forbearance,
a hand too tender

to sever lustrous life from the soil.

Two

. . . with one foot
in the old world
and one in the new . . .

Juan Picks Apples

Packs apples,
brings me apples,
green-flecked, glossy red,
big as my head, as big as I dream
of apples,
laughing in my sleep,
splitting red skin and crisp flesh
like a maul rends wood for fire.
Juan always brings me apples,
and we laugh in the garden,
separating weeds from soil,
wresting grey foliage
from green life
rising to a spring sun.
He always brings me apples,
but not today.
His mother died in Michoacán,
and he can never go back.
He crossed the border,
lapping filthy water
like a dog.
He sent money,
but her new husband
drank it down,
leaving nothing for a doctor.
He always brings me apples,
but not today.
His mother died in Michoacán,
and a great red chunk
split away from his heart.

FOREIGN

My father wandered
these same streets,
a little country boy
come to the city,
a boy who knew
pigs, cows, and ducks,
dirt roads and open fields,
not lawns and pavement.

Before he wore long pants,
my father rattled the lid
of his grandma's cracker jar,
sat on her front porch,
and pressed his nose
to the corner store window
with a penny in his hand.

He was a country boy,
lost among the cars and people,
warned of peril down the street,
Watch out! A Chinaman will get you!
One day he ran,
hot breath searing his throat,
the day he saw another,
little more alien than himself,
also walking to the store,
glossy black pigtail
swinging down his back.

Migrant Heart

Parched, earth-brown skin,
an unexplored continent,
watered with sweat,
a bronze photo holds him fast.
Sleek black hair,
sleepy dark eyes,
slow, full-lipped smile,
a young man
in a schoolroom full of children,
a twelve-year-old Tejano boy
who arrived every spring to work
in onion and asparagus fields.

On rare rainy days
Alfredo sat one row over
in a two-room school,
his blue flannel shirt still dusty
from the farm.

I moved from grade school
to middle school,
waiting each day
for him to climb aboard the bus,
but he could not follow,
he could not cross
from his world to mine.

Instead he followed the sun,
the seasons, crop to crop,
field to field.

THE ALLEY

The garden waits,
black, wet, tumescent,
opening, warming, under the sun.
Raspberries glitter crimson,
lithe poppies flutter,
and delphiniums spike
above gray paint chips,
hugging a crumbling foundation.
A spotted pit bull
barks hoarsely from a flatbed,
bass counterpoint to
a steady yap of Chihuahuas.
With dainty pink paws,
a neighbor's cat fouls the soil,
pint-sized owners demanding
her immediate return
over a blowsy wire fence.
Blocking the alley,
a young woman honks impatiently.
José Jr., jersey shorts riding low,
emerges with a house-jarring slam,
verbally fucking the world,
and they spin out, a spray of gravel
lifting behind them.

Behind Drawn Shades

The house is grimy around the edges,
dust settling into corners,
toys and clothing scattered,
dirty dishes stacking the sink.
Ana spends days in bed with her feet up,
struggling to bring a boy to the light
of a sunny spring day.

Afraid to go out, almost afraid to move,
she rolls on her side,
curling like the fetus she carries.
His life will not be like hers.
He will not be afraid to go out,
not afraid of curious stares,
not afraid because a visa expired
four years ago.

Esta Vida Querida

A tinge of frost hangs in the evening air,
blood alcohol levels, barbecue smoke, and voices
rise with red balloons.
A solitary guitar strums softly.
A ragged male chorus,
gloriously *borracho,*
sings for dear life.
Heads thrown back, they shout,
La vida, amor to the skies.

Silver horses in full gallop across the grill,
a shiny club cab stirs dust in the alley.
An accordion sighs, José cranks up the Tejano,
and music pounds at our door,
windows thumping like bass drums
as our house and his rock
to a steady oom-pah beat.
Carnitas simmer on the fire,
cerveza chills in the cooler,
and a yard full of friends laugh
and drink *tristeza* away.

Magpie Spring

I know it's spring
when sunlight glints across frosty windshields
and meadowlarks wake me,
when lime-plugged Corona bottles litter José's driveway,
when magpies reline their nest, dive-bombing the unwary,
robins trace a chain-link fence,
and pit bulls lunge the length of their chains, breath smoking the air,
when boys with prickly crew cuts belly-race down the hill on skateboards,
scouring alleys for beer bottles, to be lined up like the condemned
and smashed with round, well-chosen rocks,
when squirrels skitter up and down trees,
and pit bulls doze in the sun, snores rending the air,
when a squat plastic motorcycle blocks the sidewalk,
chalk figures in skirts holding hands under its wheels,
when Pablo's house is festooned with deflated birthday balloons,
when Mr. López scrapes the paint off his lanky old house, again,
when hammers ring from the rooftops,
big bass speakers rap until morning,
and a rooster relay summons the dawn.

PICANTE

Surprise hybrids in the garden,
tart sweetness of bell pepper
mates with jalapeño.
A firestorm of flavor
explodes in my mouth,
bringing tears to my eyes.

Parole

The phone jangles me awake.
It's Frank calling from prison.
He'll be paroled soon,
and he'd like to call our house *home.*
Drowsy, I hedge,
What are the rules?
No meth, no guns.
Suddenly street-smart,
I fire back,
deciding a disfunctional flintlock
in the closet counts.

WALKING

She walks, a white-haired apparition,
translucent skin, bone, and determination
under a straw hat.
She walks, more shuffle than step,
bending into a chill wind,
dry and brittle as the wide brim
pulled down over eyebrows pale as corn silk,
eyes clear, as sheer, as blue veins
in the back of her hand.

La Música

Disorderly optimism and muscular vitality
echo through the alleys, *en los callejones.*

I want to find the music,
be part of that bursting, riotous life,
leave my old life behind.

I want black eyes, brown skin,
a lilting language on my lips
and *alegría* in my heart.

I want to ride the crest of that wave
swamping everything before it,
claiming my old country and making it new.

But I cannot go with them.
I am the other, *la gabacha,* the white girl in the big gray house
with one foot in the old world and one in the new.

Little Mexico

Nosing through a feathered vortex of snow,
the leggy old pickup bumps along the alley,
studs digging into the ice.
The heater spits a little warmth at my feet,
and I pull my jacket up around my ears.
I flip on 97.9, *la más Mexicana.*
A bright flare of trumpets, riffle of accordion,
and hefty oom-pah beat fill the cab
as I rock through the potholes
on my way to warm tortillas, tacos
spilling chicken, onion, and avocado—
my little Mexico in the snow.

THE BUNGALOW

Grown children drag apple crates
full of chisels, pliers, and garden shears,
coffee cans full of roofing nails and bolts,
and a backbreaking cast-iron band saw
from the dusty garage onto the lawn.

Tiger-oak table, chairs, and desk roll
to the porch on balky casters,
and leavings of a life lay
for an afternoon under the sycamore tree.
Two months later, Ramón's big truck purrs

in the shade of the tree.
He installs deadbolts, bars,
and fortifies the alley with a stout metal fence.
Two men lug a black-bellied woodstove
across the porch,

and as the leaves begin to fall,
six Lilliputians lean back on ropes,
pinioning burly arms of the great sycamore.
A little man scrambles up the trunk with a chainsaw.
One by one branches meet earth,

chain-link fence,
and an unsuspecting corner
of Mrs. Wilson's house.
As Ramón and María settle in for the winter,
bricks from the chimney fall with the snow,
shattering in clouds of red dust across the frozen ground.

I Want to Die Like Fall

Isadora red-scarf sunset draping the sky,
searing wet, black earth with maple leaf paws,
fog droplets gathered in ruching around my neck.

I want to burn with crimson fever
cooled by sudden raindrops,
swell like rose hips among the thorns,
red and ripe as berries on the dogwood.

I want to die like fall,
weeping sweet nectar for each ruddy leaf that falls,
withering in a paisley of spinning leaves and twisting stems,
dying slowly, lavishly,
dropping leaves one by one,
giving up the last of the copper-gold robe,
Gypsy Rose style
to the first cold wind that blows.

Three

. . . where the wild
and the urban meet.

Intoxication

Muriendo de amor,
crying for love in the streets,
Mexican oldies spill from a slack door
of a square-jawed four-by-four,
eddying into shoals of dusk,
tossed along
on a rushing tide of spring,
a tide leaving nothing untouched,
not even the meanest branches
of thorny locusts on the hillside,
scrawny trees bursting with bloom,
cascades of creamy blossoms
tumbling from groaning branches
like Rapunzel's hair.

Even chainsaw-wracked survivors,
trees in name only, manage to bloom.
Shoots and flowers spring
from severed trunks and limbs.
Ivory petals bless my head,
dripping like honey into my hair,
rough branches interlace above,
and the dusty pathway becomes a bower,
waning light heavy with promise,
gold-white blooms
phosphorescing in darkness,
crying honey to the bees
in this world of concrete and asphalt,
making me fully as drunk
on scent-sated air
as the neighbors are on Bud.

PROHIBIDO

Soon, if he is not looking,
the neighbor on the alley
may graciously
grant me a cucumber.
Day by day,
I watch it swell,
plump, mirror-sheen green,
prickly, glossy, full-bellied.
I watch patiently
as starlings wait
for strawberries.
I watch the vine
weave over, around,
fluted buds slipping under,
through chain-link,
opening to the sun,
teasing with promise
of pale, translucent flesh,
vernal kaleidoscope,
a wheeling galaxy
of rotating seeds.

Second Story

The neighbor wheezes
with each step
on the groaning stairs,
pausing to sit aloft,
a life observed,
watching, measuring other lives
as her own dwindles away.

Alone these forty years,
she yet understands
the wordless dialect
of a man and woman
who chance to meet
in the yard below.

The young woman
lowers her eyes
as the man traces
a triangle in the dust
with his boot.

He glances over
his shoulder
at boisterous children
playing in the street.

The two laugh,
a little too loudly,
and from her lofty perch,
the neighbor peers down
into the stealthy hearts of lovers.

Front-Porch Lothario

Burly Buddha of the front porch,
basks in the sun, meditating, dozing.
Traffic, neighbors swirl around him.
Eyes half open, he waits for long shadows
to hide furtive footsteps, waiting
for long shadows to fall over the back porch
of a tumble-down house around the corner,
a little hovel that finally surrenders to the flames,
torched by firefighters who never knew
it already smoldered with afternoon *amor.*

LENGUA

Brimful of tamales
and tacos de *lengua*,
comfortable around the table,
we blend Spanish and English,
slipping in and out.
They laugh, *You can go*
to Mexico.
They will think you are Mexican.

I hope so, I say.
They will ask
for your green card
at the border,
and then you will need
a coyote.
Juan laughs raucously,
Oh, wait! That's my story.

Vine Street Underpass

A white froth of spirea spills down the hillside,
over a chain-link fence marking the freeway.
Sparrows and squirrels chatter
in ancient, untrimmed trees—
brittle branches twisting toward the sun
chartreuse-crowned with the hope of spring.

A homeless man, like the birds,
has made his nest here, wrapped in a torn afghan
on a bed of pine needles, cradled
in a chain-link hammock against the hill.

Overhead, a tattered plastic bag dangles from a branch.
Pink apricot petals dust the asphalt pathway,
broken beer bottles sparkle amber in the sun.
Giant dandelions flourish untamed,
and a free-range housecat hunkers down in the grass,
stalking an errant cottontail.

As the sun rises, the homeless man moves on,
and I, alone, am left to find
the unlucky rabbit's foot
on a narrow path where the wild and the urban meet.

Urban Stew

A stray tabby paws the soil,
at once sullying and enriching
black humus in our flowerbeds.

A wayward skinhead moves into
a vacant garage across the alley,
marking his territory who-knows-where.

Detritus builds up, rotting, fermenting,
a compost of stray cats and humanity.

OF EVERY FEATHER

I step into a garden
of late-blooming roses,
a morning for birds—
geese braying across the sky,
doves dipping delicate heads,
birds lining lilac branches
and the lip of the fountain,
beaks profiled in sun-shadow,
all nations, sharp-eyed starling,
fat frowsy robin, trim gray finch,
waking and foraging together.

QUIZÁS

The bull bursts from darkness
into a blaze of magenta and gold,
sequins and silk.
The matador plays the melody of instinct,
reckless and rhythmic, cunning and cruel—
pivot, half turn, full serpentina.
Bewildered, the bull lowers his horns,
probing the mystery again and again.
At last, the two come together,
bonding in bright and bloody moments
under the cape.
The bull staggers,
swaying to the chant of the crowd,
the call of the trumpet,
bowing at last to the song of the cape.
Does the matador love the bull?
Quizás.

Fiesta of Trees

Trees, green, orange, red, and gold,
unfurl crinkled skirts on a breeze
singing through the branches.
Leaves like golden Monarchs
from forests of Michoacán
take wing and flutter down—
a field of dawn
in a darkening world.

Ubiquitous

Safeway carts everywhere—
abandoned in alleys,
lolling in backyards,
reclining insouciantly
among the weeds,
upended, wheels spinning
aimlessly in the breeze,
even tête-à-tête,
metal muzzle to muzzle
under mossy-barked locusts.

A veritable wardrobe
rests beside the pathway,
a single high-topped boot,
lost, strayed, or parted in anger
from its mate,
pants, too, in rumpled, running pose,
jacket crumpled into dukes up,
fighting stance,
and a pink, barely-pubescent bra,
edged in black lace, lies
in tousled, yellowed grass of the hillside,
cupping clouds and sky.

Not-quite-discarded couches
fray on porches, in pickups,
and under ancient trees.
Inside and out,
big-screen TVs flicker
through the night.
Mixed packs of dogs,
tiny dust mop mutts
and pampered Chihuahuas,
fearless behind wire fences,

nip one another for the honor
of chiding me as I pass.

Countless beer bottles
seek solitude on porch sills,
curbs, and in open doorways,
or simply gather in forgetful groups
on sunlit grass the morning after.

SMILING AT MEN

English class is over,
and Mario calls her,
voice rising
on a lilt of irritation.
It's late, he says,
imagining an inexorable
downhill slope,
Lorena going to class,
smiling at men,
leaving with one.

Third

All smiles, Mario calls to the street,
Come and see the baby.
Lorena hands me a scowling baby,
clenched like an angry fist,
third in an unlucky succession of girls.
Lorena's mother, small, indigenous,
newly imported from Mexico,
gazes balefully at my baseball cap,
sweats, and running shoes.
As I greet her in halting Spanish,
she shrinks deeper into the sunken couch,
and I hand the baby off
the minute she starts to squall.

. . . relics
of a hardscrabble
life . . .

Four

Apricot Down

Between cuts, between branches,
Juan pirouettes on tiptoe,
spry as a squirrel in tennis shoes,
perching, then straddling,
balancing a lethal whir
of chainsaw above him.

Somewhere down the alley,
Pepe Aguilar sings of broken hearts,
and the chainsaw bites deep,
branches raining down
as white petals and golden fruit once did.

Rough ridges of the great trunk
resist, inertia born of earth
and fifty years of sleet and snow,
but my sylvan Venus has lost
more than one arm now,
sharp metal teeth singing through
sap and heartwood.

Eight hours and two chainsaws later,
enthusiasm wanes with the dusk,
and between beers,
Juan struggles with a two-foot stump
as three friends gather round
to eat, drink, and offer advice.
Later our derelict van
rolls off into the darkness,
uninsured as the day it was made.

As the van trundles away,

the stump waits in darkness
and another day in rain.
At dawn on a third misty day,
a squirrel with cheeks
full of apricot kernels
jerks to attention.

A little Chevy pickup sputters and smokes, idling
while Juan grinds the base of the stump,
sharpening, meditating between cuts.
The transmission whines, wheels spinning trenches,
drawing rope taut to almost breaking.
With one great crack, the stump breaks free,
ricocheting across frost-spiked ground,
thudding to a stop.

I stand in the dark circle of soil
in what was once shade under her branches,
a grave of trampled black, ringed
with shattered limbs and sawdust,
and I grieve,
shamelessly, in this small loss,
for all my losses,
all the dark graves of sundered earth
no hand can ever smooth.

WILDLIFE EXPRESS

Puffing like a locomotive,
Ramón's chimney belches
gray clouds of smoke,
and neither sharp December air
nor firefighters can quell it.
Ever the canny businessman,
Ramón drafts immigrants
from his ramshackle rentals,
workers desperate enough to barter.
Unpaid work crews come and go,
tearing out plumbing, wiring,
at last abandoning their tools in disgust.

And so the house
returns to the wild,
the yard, a field of foxtails,
thronging with crickets
who are never silent.
The country has come to the city,
golden in the August sun,
like a wheat field ready for harvest.
The back door gapes,
screen propped open
by a fallen gutter,
curious cats strolling
in and out at will.

With city inspectors closing in,
Ramón hires a real crew,
a crew complete with
compressor, nail guns,
rickety truck, and blaring boom-box.
A crew that not only roofs the house
but dances a tool belt Cumbia

on an oriented strand board,
a crew with Yankee know-how,
gangsta pants, conquistador beards,
and pizza and Coke for lunch.

Feral

A testosterone-charged yowl
knifes through our sleep
as Big Daddy lays claim
to prime bird-hunting turf,
leaving paw prints
and a pungent message
on our back steps.

Ruthless and street-savvy,
he haunts our nights,
an orange-maned marauder
demanding food and fealty,
slinking in and out
of fire-blasted, rock-shattered
vacant houses,
prowling the garden,
furtively lapping water
from the fountain
and silently treading
the unpainted porch
beneath our bedroom window.

Our adolescent tomcat,
no match for the ring-tailed terror
of this or any other block,
retreats, ceding our yard
and a large clump of fur.

Finches desert the lilacs
as the big cat decrees
an end to birdsong.
His hubris knows
no bounds until
one morning

he crouches, silent,
biding his time,
lifting his regal head,
to glare with sullen amber eyes,
nose rutted and scarred,
no one's prissy
housebroken kitty,
epic urban warrior
beguiled now
by an artless Trojan Horse,
a simple wire cage,
and a plate of tuna.

THE LAST NINETY-YEAR-OLD ON THE BLOCK

Mamie tends her house, her garden
better than herself,
making the truck route bloom
as culture and language
ebb and flow around her.
She swings a hammer,
wields paintbrush and hoe,
fixing, digging, weeding.

Eyes crinkled with sun
and pleasure,
shovel in hand,
she leads me
through a forest
of delphinium and foxglove,
hollyhock and hosta.
Ya need one of these, Kid,
she says, uprooting
 a spiny nest
of red-skirted poppies.

She broke one day,
hip cracking
like a shovel handle in the rain.
An ambulance carried her off
to dark hallways
without flowers or sun,
shovels or shears,
a handful of leathery leaves
still clutched in her palm.

Poppies still flourish,
and foxglove bloom without surcease
in my garden and in the garden
she left behind.

Orgullo

Mario slams down the phone.
He won't work for him again.
English class is for children.
He won't go there again.
After all, he has his pride.
Until Lorena asks,
Can you fold it in your pocket?
Can you fill your stomach with it?
Can you feed your children with it?

New Neighbors

The tailgate opens
like a horn of plenty,
abundance flowing onto the porch
and into the yard,
old tires, mismatched shoes,
amorphous mattress
propped beside the front door.
A square-grilled F-150 lists
under a Linden tree,
water running to rainbow
beneath the crankcase,
bare-metal bed mounded
with boxes brimful
of worn towels and stuffed animals,
pleading paws extended,
sodden after three days of rain.

Bittersweet

Mario is a rueful survivor,
his ten-year-old faith shattered
in an piñata accident at the height
of the Posadas party season
in Jalisco.

After too many cups of *ponche,*
the man holding the rope
loosed his grip,
and instead of a sweet taste of *dulces*
dribbling down his chin,
Mario reels from the crack of an *olla,*
tasting a salty trickle of blood
from his forehead.

Cars and four-wheeled rigs line the street,
pink and blue balloons trace the porch,
and a pig-tailed piñata floats overhead,
a piñata with silver streamers
for Sofía's fifth birthday,
her pink dress, a swirl of cotton candy,
Sofía of the black pigtails,
Sofía watching
a piñata dip and roll among the clouds,
daring a blindfolded child
to crack the magic open
with one wild swing of a bat,
Sofía's own silvery flight of fancy
with Mario, her papá,
steadying the rope.

Vanquished

Broken from years
on the meat-cutting floor,
the old man cries
with pain in his sleep,
so Ana calls
the next morning,
struggling to clothe
his unwilling limbs,
shadow his halting steps.

At the desk,
she sputters with indignation,
gasping for words
as if they were air,
accent sharpened
by stress and fear.

Insolent, the receptionist
denies her error,
on an English battlefield
where she will prevail.
Impassive, uncomprehending,
the old man waits,
but the doctor will not
see him today.
And others who wait,
ignorant of humiliation
in another language,
stare at Ana and her father
as they make their retreat.

IMPOSTERS

Pale pretenders have taken over their house,
eating in their kitchen,
sleeping in their bedroom,
shouting at their children in English,
vowels slapping against hard consonants,
not the smooth, *dulce* syrup of Spanish.
I will never know their names,
and I will not forgive them soon.

Fifth-Wheel Lovers

Cheeks hollow
from a half century
of inhaling,
the old woman withers,
lugging an oxygen tank
from room to room.

One by one, worn,
middle-aged children
straggle in to care for her,
first a dented travel trailer
with curling metal trim,
then a battered fifth-wheel,
four scruffy, barking mutts
patrolling the perimeter.

White trash, I think,
somehow not deserving
of a door that locks,
windows that latch,
and a furnace that warms.

But as I watch,
one son mows tall grass
with his good left arm,
while others clear away
relics of a hardscrabble life,
lawn mowers, parked where they died,
tires, batteries, fenders,
shovels and hoes,
tools for working the earth,
claimed by the earth.

Framed in my window,
the youngest daughter and
her fifth-wheel lover swelter
in the shade of a mattress,
drape laundry over the fence,
quarrel and sleep in the open.

Unhinged,
the fifth-wheel door swings wide,
the lover tossed blinking
into the morning light,
reduced from five wheels
to two, pedaling furiously
down the alley, dodging words
thrown after him like rocks,
Don't you ever
put your hands on me again!

Hammering apace,
the workmen next door
take no notice,
not then nor later
when the exile vaults the fence,
slipping inside to retrieve
boxers, t-shirts, socks,
fleeing down the alley
with one last backward glance.

Three nights later,
struggling to silence
the gravel under our feet,
we stumble on them near the alley
spread out on the grass under the stars,
her head resting in the crook of his arm.

Mrs. America

I grapple in the heat
with procrastination
and pink-legged pigweeds,
towering like California palms,
spiky grasses headed like wheat,
puncture vine and mallow
bonded fiercely to parched earth
along the alley.

By the time I finish,
a great sheaf
of seed-laden weeds
spills from my arms
as I make my stately progress
down my own sidewalk runway
crowned with sweat and a tie-dyed
baseball cap.

CROSSING

His mouth full
of broken syllables,
Mario dies a death
with each twisted word
he utters,
each turn of phrase,
a mark of difference.
Powerful in Spanish,
he is captive, subjugated
in manacles of English.
Still struggling
with his twenty-year adversary,
he asks me,
When you speak Spanish,
do you feel empty?
No, I say,
I feel full, llena de amor,
llena de posibilidades.
But I do not live or die,
drown or thrive,
by this language,
as he does by English.
I do not face daily
small humiliations.
I can cross the border
freely, *sin pena.*

Glossary

abuela: grandmother

alegría: joy

amor: love

bisabuelos: great-grandparents

borracho: drunk

callejones: alleys, *en los callejones*: in the alleys

carnitas: literally "little meats," is a Mexican dish from the state of Michoacán. Carnitas are made by braising or simmering pork in oil or lard for three to four hours until tender. The meat is served with chopped coriander leaves (*cilantro*), diced onion, salsa, guacamole, tortillas, and refried beans (*frijoles refritos*) [Source: https://en.wikipedia.org/wiki/Carnitas]

la casa: house

cerveza: beer

Cumbia: a dance-oriented music genre popular throughout Latin America. It began as a courtship dance practiced among the African population on the Caribbean coast of Colombia and Panama and is now one of the most widespread and unifying musical genres to emerge from Latin America. [Source: https://en.wikipedia.org/wiki/Cumbia]

dar a luz: to give birth, literally to give to the light

de: of

dulce: sweet

dulces: sweets or candies

esperanza: hope

esta: this

gabacho (masculine), **gabacha** (feminine): a word used in the Spanish language to describe foreigners of different origins. In the United States, it is a pejorative term used by Chicanos for white Americans. It is not widely used or understood by Spanish-speakers in the Americas outside of the United States and Mexico. [Source: https://en.wikipedia.org/wiki/Gabacho]

la más Mexicana: the most Mexican (radio station)

lengua: tongue or language

lleno (masculine)**, llena** (feminine): full

muriendo: dying

muriendo de amor: dying of love

olla: a clay pot used to form the body of a piñata

orgullo: pride

pena: shame, punishment, troubles, or struggle

picante: spicy or hot

ponche: alcoholic beverage, punch

Las Posadas: a novenario (nine days of religious observance) celebrated chiefly in Mexico and by Mexican-Americans in the Southwestern United States, beginning December 16 and ending December 24, on evenings (about 8 or 10 PM), during which Mexican families participate in nightly Christmas processions that re-create the Holy Pilgrimage of Mary, Joseph and the baby Jesus on their way to Bethlehem. [Source: https://en.wikipedia.org/wiki/Las_Posadas]

posibilidades: possibilities, opportunities

prohibido: forbidden

querida: dear

quizás: perhaps

sin: without

Tejano: a resident of Texas of Criollo Spanish or Mexican American descent. [Source: https://en.wikipedia.org/wiki/Tejano]

> 1. a Texan of Hispanic descent

> 2. [probably short for *conjunto tejano*, literally, Texan ensemble]: Tex-Mex popular music combining elements of traditional, rock, polka, and country music and often featuring an accordion. [Source: http://www.merriam-webster.com/dictionary/Tejano]

tristeza: sadness

la vida: life

Acknowledgments

Lynn gratefully acknowledges the following publications in which these poems first appeared:

"La Casa de Mis Bisabuelos" first appeared in *Poets on the Coast* anthology (2013).

"Golden Eye" was first published in *Poeming Pigeons: Poems about Birds* (The Poetry Box, 2015).

"Magpie Spring", first appeared in *Poets on the Coast* anthology (2016).

"La Música" was previously published in T*he Poeming Pigeon: Poems about Music* (The Poetry Box, 2016).

PRAISE FOR GIVING GROUND

Giving Ground inhabits a world of concrete and blossoms, margins where cultures meet and languages strive to make sense of one another. Author Lynn Knapp displays gentle humor and the heartfelt urge to understand, to cross the border of difference in a neighborhood of alleys, music, chain link fences, and "sunlit grass the morning after."

~ Linda Andrews
Author, *Escape of the Bird Women*

Giving Ground is an invitation to be part of the neighborhood. In these narrative poems, Lynn Knapp observes the natural (flora & fauna) and human relationships happening around her. Accessible and engaging, these poems make us feel as if we are standing on the porch looking out into the small town where "robins and finches forage together" and "a yard full of friends laugh." Walk down the path with the poet and meet the world taking place around you.

~ Kelli Russell Agodon
Author, *Hourglass Museum* & *The Daily Poet*

In Lynn Knapp's new collection *Giving Ground,* myriad forms of life abound – animals, plants, flowers, and immigrants – transplants from Mexico. Vivid natural imagery becomes the backdrop for a unique set of characters who fight for survival, alternately shocking and amusing the reader. Yet there's a rare tenderness apparent in this small-town world, a place where food, music, and language come from a foreign land but are assimilated without question, perhaps because there is never the luxury of a choice.

~ Judith Skillman
Author of *Storm*
Winner, Eric Mathieu King Fund Award

In *Giving Ground*, Lynn Knapp explores the interstices of the controlled and the wild in her garden and her neighborhood. The nature trail near her house is bordered by railroad tracks and a highway, is populated by half-domestic rabbits, descendants of a runaway pet, and homeless campers. Knapp pulls weeds from her own garden and finds flowers blooming in an abandoned one, observes her neighbors from the vantage of windows, alleys, and the passage of time. We sense a desire to close those gaps between herself and those around her, to no longer be la gabacha in her neighborhood, but to pull her friends and neighbors – and their joys and traditions – into full citizenship in her world.

~ Teri Zipf
Author, *Outside the School of Theology*
William Stafford Memorial Award in Poetry

In *Giving Ground*, Lynn M. Knapp draws us into a world where "the wild and the urban meet." The narrator, "the white girl in the big gray house," guides us through neighborhoods where English – and Spanish – speakers share the landscape with rabbits, birds, and feral cats; where hardworking parents live beside "grownup gangstas," and where proud men like Mario suffer "daily/ small humiliations" because they cannot speak English fluently.

Combining deft portraits of both past and current inhabitants with lyrical nature poems, Knapp reflects the demographic shifts that define American history. The house that a German great-grandpa built becomes a *casa* painted aqua blue. Now "pale pretenders" who shout "at their children in English ... not the smooth, *dulce* syrup of Spanish" have arrived. The ground keeps giving way – and this sharp-eyed, talented poet captures that unchanging truth in a moving, finely-crafted collection.

~ Carolyn Martin
Author, *The Way a Woman Knows*

About The Author

Lynn M. Knapp is a poet, memoirist, teacher, and musician. She lives in a hundred-year-old house and walks every day in one of the oldest neighborhoods in the Pacific Northwest. The grit, grime, and unexpected beauty of the central city inspire her life and her writing. Her poetry has appeared in *The Burden of Light: Poems on Illness and Loss* (2014), *The Poeming Pigeon* and *The Lost River Review* (2015). Her work also appears online at the Museum of Northwest Art in La Conner, Washington.

ABOUT THE POETRY BOX®

The Poetry Box® was founded in 2011 by Shawn Aveningo & Robert R. Sanders, who whole-heartedly believe that every day spent with the people you love, doing what you love, is a moment in life worth celebrating. It all started out as our way to help people memorialize the special milestones in their lives by melding custom poems with photographic artwork for anniversaries, birthdays, holidays and other special occasions. Robert and Shawn expanded on their shared passion for creating poetry and art with the introduction of The Poetry Box® Book Publishing.

As Robert and Shawn continue to celebrate the talents of their fellow artisans and writers, they now offer professional book design and publishing services to poets looking to publish their collections of poems.

And as always, The Poetry Box® believes in giving back to the community. Each month a portion of all sales will benefit a different charity. For a complete list of the charities currently supported, please visit the Giving Back page on their website at www.ThePoetryBox.com.

Feel free to visit The Poetry Box® online bookstore, where you'll find more books including:

Keeping It Weird: Poems & Stories of Portland, Oregon

Verse on the Vine: A Celebration of Community, Poetry, Art & Wine

The Way a Woman Knows by Carolyn Martin

Of Course, I'm a Feminist! edited by Ellen Goldberg

Poeming Pigeons: Poems about Birds

The Poeming Pigeon: Poems about Food

The Poeming Pigeon: Doobie or Not Doobie?

The Poeming Pigeon: Poems about Music

and more ...

Order Form

Need more copies for friends and family? No problem. We've got you covered with two convenient ways to order:

1. Go to our website at www.thePoetryBox.com and click on Bookstore.

or

2. Fill out the order form. Email it to Shawn@thePoetryBox.com

Name: _____

Shipping Address: _____

_____

Phone Number: (____) _____

Email Address: _____@_____

Payment Method: __Cash __Check __PayPal Invoice __Credit Card

Credit Card #: _____ CCV _____

Expiration Date: _____ Signature: _____

Giving Ground by Lynn M. Knapp

# of Copies: _____

x $12.00: _____

Plus Shipping & Handling: _____
($3 per book, or $7.95 for 3 or more books)

Order Total: _____

Thank You!

Made in the USA
Columbia, SC
13 October 2017